The Voice *of the* Healer

Then and Now

*Expressions of written prayers,
described in poetic form,
accompanied by Scriptural references
and evocative imagery*

Amelia Brumm

Amelia Brumm
2006

All photographs (with the exception of the photograph on page 14) are from the personal collections of Dr. Lynn F. Brumm and Dr. Evan J. Boote.

Pleasant Word (a division of WinePress Publishing, PO Box 428, Enumclaw, WA 98022) functions only as book publisher. As such, the ultimate design, content, editorial accuracy, and views expressed or implied in this work are those of the author.

Scripture references marked RSV are taken from the Revised Standard Version, 1881, 1895, 1901, 1952

Scripture references marked MSG are taken from the The Message, ©2002, Eugene H. Peterson.

ISBN 1-4141-0603-3
Library of Congress Catalog Card Number: 2005909810

Dedication

With deep love
To my devoted husband, Lynn,
our daughter, Nancy Lee
and son-in-law, Evan
without whom this book of prayers
could not have become alive

*It is good for me
to have been afflicted;
so that I may learn
your statutes.*

Psalm 119:71

Special Recognition

To my precious family members who were my source of encouragement in their persistence, and nudged me forward to publish my work. To my husband for his advice, undying patience, and confidence in me when I felt a sense of inadequacy. To our daughter for her gentle spirit and clear discernment when I needed guidance — her walk in Christ brought a deeper mother-daughter relationship. To our son-in-law for his quiet demeanor, and his forever patience in the preparation of this manuscript. To each of them whom I deeply love, I am eternally grateful. To Christine Sheriff for her willingness to diligently proofread my writings, which was a monumental task. To Reverend Gordon Dahnke who believed in me and patiently encouraged my heart — for his counsel and valuable comments, I will always be grateful.

To my Mentor and Helper, the ministry of the Holy Spirit who helped me weave the different threads of prayer into the art of poetry. To my teacher who taught me compassion and sensitivity to identify with a hurting human race and how to seek scripture references to further aid their hurting hearts. To each of you, my heartfelt thanks. Each of you, with your own unique talents, is a treasured gift sent to me in my times of need.

Amelia Brumm

Explication

By way of introduction, I have given considerable thought about how to represent these expressions of prayers through written poetry.

Please allow me to share with you my struggle as a chronic pain sufferer. Through a series of many incidents over a twelve-year span, an unexpected, unknown stranger slowly and insidiously invaded every area of my body, mind and spirit. This unwanted intruder took me on a long voyage into the valley of hopelessness and into a deep, lingering, persistent despair. During these prolonged, overwhelming, distressed years I was shrouded in weariness with no relief of pain. I began to pen the deep pain-filled feelings. My collection of writings is the result of my pain expressed in prayer through the art of poetry. For me, prayer and poetry became wedded together. Soon I became soaked in scriptural references. Both prayer and poetry together have deepened my personal relationship in Christ.

Many are surprised when pain, losses and sorrows happen, be it physical, emotional, mental, spiritual or all four. Today we live in a broken world. Not one of us is exempt from hurtful feelings that wound the heart. My writings have a two-fold purpose.

First: Primarily, they focus on those afflicted with suffering — seeking words of encouragement in their times of need, a measure of comfort, increased strength and peace.

Second: To bring those who travel a godless, purposeless life, lost in a vacuous wasteland, to turn around and seek a Savior in Christ. Who? Not a stranger but a compassionate friend. *"... and it shall be that everyone who calls on the name of the Lord will be saved"* (Acts 2:21).

My heartfelt prayer to those who suffer multi-health issues is not to lose heart, be discouraged or dismayed. Put aside self, offer up your pain to those in need and rest in the assurance and security of God's gracious mercy and love. In terms of wholeness, from the medical perspective, be enlightened to both the medical professionals and to the promises of God's grace. By integrating the physical and the spiritual, they both work toward your inner healing.

It is my strong belief that these inspirational expressions are as relative in our hurting broken world as they were two thousand years ago. Each expression is based on scriptural truths and messages of grace.

"Beloved, do not be surprised at the fiery ordeal which comes upon you to prove you, as though something strange were happening to you. But rejoice in so far as you share Christ's suffering, that you may also rejoice and be glad when his glory is revealed" (1 Peter 4:12,13).

The Resurrection Breakfast

Come, an open invitation
      to the Resurrection Breakfast.
The messenger, your resurrection host,
      requests the honor of your presence.
      A get-together on the shores of Galilee.
All that hunger and thirst, please come to converse
      with your dearest Friend, your companion, Sir!
Come, you are graciously invited. Why?
      To gather for the Great Fish Fry.
For anyone who eats and drinks with Him, the Christ
      abides in Him and He in you.
All gather about the communion feast,
      A communal seaside feast of peace.
Together to enjoy an intimate personal time,
      for it is He. "It is the Lord!" The Bread of Life,
      the One who taught, lived, loved and died,
      buried and arose, the True Vine, His Father to be glorified.
As we depart, as He ascends, He gives His last command:
      Drop in your cast net, be Catchers,
      fishers of men, spiritual food to be fed.
      Shore up to the pull of life, separate bad from the good.
"This is my commandment, that you love
      one another as I have loved You."
      "I give to you another Counselor, the spirit of truth...
      who will guide you into all truth."

April 3, 2003

John 21:9-14; John 15:4-11; John 21:7; Matthew 4:19-22; Matthew 13:47,48;
John15:12; John16:13

Contents

Expressions of Healing Prayers

Reflections of God's High Calling of Suffering.
If we suffer with Him, we shall reign with Him

O, Jesus, My Joy

O, Jesus, my joy,
to you I pray.
From the lips of my mouth
I should like to say,
"Thank you," for the gift of joy.
It's morning dawn,
the evening fades away.
Shouts!
A festal burst of cheer
breaks out - a solo anew
a day of gladness brand-new. [1]
Dressed in beams of light
flowing through my life
like a bubbling brook
humming cheerfully along,
a joyous singing song.
O, Jesus, my abounding joy,
continue to pursue me
as you do in your tender way.
Help me to lean more on you,[2]
you alone, in all I do.
Grant to me a patient heart
the kind like the farmer waiting
to receive the early and latter rains.[3]

Not to go my carnal way.
Instead,
trusting you to move ahead
to do my best
to go for you
to do what you
gave me to do.
Grant to me a larger, humble heart
-the kind like yours,
to wash another's feet.[4]
Clothe me in a servant's garb
to clearly show what I should be -
what you have unselfishly done for
me.
And Jesus, my true joy,
What do I say
to those when confronted with bread
of tears,
with unexpected tribulations
which might seem hard to bear,
unable to lie down without fear.
"Lend me your ear, my child."
The door to my heart
opens wide
for therein lies my joy
inside.

"Come unto me, I will give you rest,"[5]
whereby unfailing joy
resides.
In quietude find your strength[6]
like the bubbling, cheerful brook
smiles cheerfully its joyous song,
bubbling clear living waters
quenching, refreshing, trilling along.[7]
O, Joy! O, Sorrow!
Shouts of joy - cries of tears
such a mixed blessing.
Times of gladness - earthly sadness
join in wedded,
present pain - eternal happiness.[8]
I will shout, Rejoice! Glory be!
Bringing in bushels of joy - to you
from me.[9]
O Jesus, my Restorer,[10]
it is you I serve – yes!
It is you I love, my Joy, my Adorer.

June 22, 2004

---

1 Psalm 100:1,2
2 Proverbs 3:5,6
3 James 5:7,8

4 John 13:5-7

5 Matthew 11:28,29
6 Nehemiah 8:10
7 John 7:37,38
8 1 Peter 5:10
9 Psalm 126:5,6
10 Psalm 80:5-7

Redemptive Suffering

When suffering with Christ
    lift up your sorrows to Him.
It works for your healing,
    your salvation, forgiveness of sin.
Blessed Redeemer, His redemptive power
    gives to us a measure of Himself
To bear the pain, to persevere,
    to honor others above ourselves.
His healing grace reaches out, touches,
    comforts us with His comforting love.
Living with suffering, He does not spare us
    with His power, enables us to know His trust.
To yield, inwardly, a sense of purity and peace
    His enrichment of character that does not cease.
This test of fire - He sits as the Father's Refiner
    to purify a faith, a Holiness, as the Purifier.
Redemptive Servant, name above all names,
    only begotten Son of God, merciful One,
Your work upon the cross revealed
    your wounded body; now, we are healed.

February 2, 2003
Psalm 66:10; Romans 5:3,4; Isaiah 53:5; 1 Peter 2:24

The Calling of the Rainbow in the Sky

Sickness, grief, suffering, the road of sorrows -
     troubled times come to us all.
Be strong, courageous, to face many tomorrows.
     He gives spiritual stamina to stand up tall.
Look to the Giver of Strength, see His gracious face.
     He tells us many things about His saving grace.
Meet Him and see, this loving, restoring One
     Who offers showered blessings from above.
When in your time of disorder or despair
     open the window of faith in prayer.
Never will He leave you; He cares -
     always near, always there.
Along with the sunshine, there must be
     droplets of rain, that sing patterns of pain.
When the sun-shower cloudburst wept a quick tear
     Behold! Also beamed a brilliant bow to wear.
God's calling of the rainbow, weaving radiant ribbons
     of hope, peace, earthly and heavenly love,
Raiments of many colors, a sign of assurance
     brightly shines, its beauty from high above.
To forget puddles of miseries, this bow in the sky
     brings an unconditional promise of comfort and hope.
A reminder of the calling of eternal love,
     made between Him and you; long ago, "two by two."

March 11, 2003
Genesis 9:13-17

The Toucher of Souls:

I heard a reassuring voice.
It seemed to say,
"If I just touch His clothes
I will be healed."
"Who touched my clothes?[1]
Woman,
your faith has healed you.
Go in peace and be freed
from your suffering."
His healing power
went out of Him,
touched her that very hour,
and made her whole.

Beloved children, come!
Only I can penetrate your
cry of throbbing, burning pain.
Soak yourselves in hope[2]
in my rejuvenating power.
Hope will not disappoint you.
Receive my healing touch this very hour.
Rejoice!
For if you suffer with me, now[3]
you shall be glorified with me, then.
I am your Resurrection One:
Listen! Suffering and rejoicing
go hand in hand. Yes!
They are one and the same.
Listen my children!
Listen to the homelessness,[4]
the kind of homelessness felt
in the Garden of Loneliness.

Intensely praying - hear the strong tears?
Dropped through the sweat of blood,
bringing forth resurrected power,
bringing forth my glory this very hour.

I am your Redeemer Healer:
Through our threaded bond
evoke a Samaritan touch -

1 Mark 5:27-34
2 Romans 5:3-7
3 1 Peter 1:6,7
4 Luke 22:39-44

14

Then and Now

tender mercies, compassion, empathy,
sympathetic feelings, all mine,
now as it was then.
My therapeutic medicines –
the greatest,
believing faith
shouldered through my precious grace,[5]
my gift, lovingly wrapped
for you eternally to embrace.

Lord, Lover of Mankind,
Living Benefactor, reverberates,
echoes that reached then.
Sandaled shoes, walking along the desert roads[6]
your presence among
     the bustling, moving crowds
your preaching along
     the tawny sands of Galilee,
teaching on the open country hillsides.
Your truth, forgiveness, and humility.

You walked through the corridors of our minds
on crooked byways, back-road highways,
through the channeled seaways
straight into our human hearts.
Your tender kindness, perpetual immensity
touching, healing our humanity
then as it is now.

You stretched out your healing hand[7]
bound up the broken-hearted,
placed miracles upon the land,[8]
cured the cripples and the lame,[9]
outcasts who lived with leprosy,[10]
those troubled by their spirits,[11]
the injured, the deaf and dumb[12]
the blind once again to see[13]
then as it is now.

5 Ephesians 2:8,9
6 Luke 6:17-19
7 Psalm 147:3
8 John 11:38-44
9 Matthew 12:22
10 Luke 17:11-19
11 Mark 9:14-29
12 Mark 7:31-37
13 Mark 10:46-52

Lord of Glory:
God of all grace, one among the wounded crowds
found your comfort for my sorrows
now and for the then tomorrows.
Yes! Lack of belief -
sought your blessed holy face.
Dressed in rags of sins - turned around,
clothed myself with your truth of grace.
My expectant heart now stretching toward
your door of glory,
     your temple home, my reward.[14]

Redeeming Freer,
continue with the move of your hand,
your soul-stirring touch,
the offer of your redemptive creed.
The sallow-faced woman like so long ago -
her persistent faith - I too, do believe.
Your fellowship of redemptive,
    healing power
touched me and I was freed
  - that very hour.

Thank you, my Redeemer Lord.
Thank you for pursuing me,
thank you for adopting me.
In the suffering I saw you more
like I never did before, my Lord.
"Behold the old has passed away (then).[15]
Now, "the new has come" to stay.
June 1, 2004

14 1 Peter 5:10-11
15 2 Corinthians 5:17

15

Through the Jumping Rope — The Trinity

Female friends – "the three"
　　Two, one at each end;
　　the third, high-stepping, then the bend
　　to the center, through the jumping rope,
　　carefree jumping with their girlish grins.
Jumping to the rhythm of a rhyme
　　testing balance, keeping time.
　　So like a child, jumping for joy -
　　this jumping rope, a newfound toy.
Best of friends forever lasting — "the three,"
　　now God's faithful women of loyalty.
　　No longer the jumping children of glee,
　　no longer the girlish likeness,
　　Christ-like more,
　　abiding in Christian lightness.
Jumping now, for the joy of the Lord[1] -
　　a newfound hope
　　found through the toy
　　of the jumping rope.
Deeply connected, together united
　　in work and play.
　　Should the center mark be missed
　　and one is down,
　　should stumble, trip or fall,
　　the other always there[2]
　　to reach, to lift that one tall.

The way of the Lord, always there,
　　lovingly to reach, to lift, to embrace
　　in His tender care, His precious grace,
　　to raise us every time we fall.
In the game of rope-jumping made of three
　　taught life's lesson -
　　to trust, to believe
　　to help, to comfort,
　　to rescue those in need.
　　Depend on Him as He depends on us
　　should be our plea.

1 Nehemiah 8:10
2 Ecclesiastes 4:10

Rope-jumping needed three,
　　one at each end - the other to jump,
　　to become one from all three,
　　as the Father, Son, and Holy Spirit
　　all three in One, the Trinity
　　both the same, both needed to
　　bring to completion a good work (do)[3]
　　needed to rise to heights eternity.
Thus, 'tis hard to break this golden thread of three.[4]
　　Thus, this rope of three - the jumping rope
　　this rope of three -
　　　　the Father, Son and Holy Ghost,
　　'tis hard to break.
　　Blest be the (mutual) tie that binds
　　　　our hearts in Christian love,[5]
　　the sacred bond of love sent from above.
Thus faith, hope, and love abide, "these three,"
　　the greatest of these is love.[6]

January 1, 2004

3 Philippians 1:6
4 Ecclesiastes 4:9
5 Blest Be the Tie that Binds,
　　Farwell, John (1740-1817)
6 1 Corinthians 13:13 (RSV)

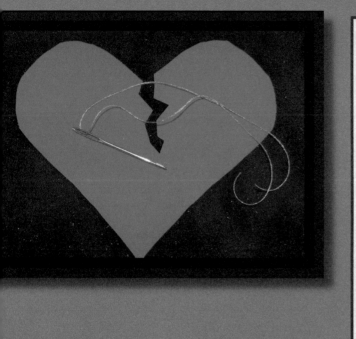

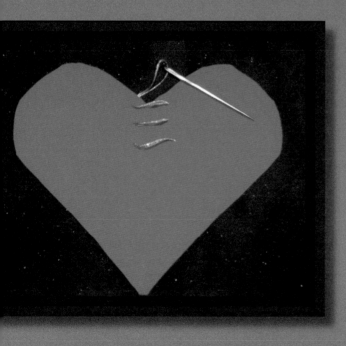

A Mended Heart

She possessed this thing of beauty
*   to behold.*
This thing once was broken,
*   now valued, now her own.*
Places in her life
*   when a maiden fair*
Gladness for sadness felt,
*   the need of emptiness to share.*
Offering up this gift of love
*   caused her heart to care.*
Like a broken vessel,
*   this inner healing altar, in need of repair.*
This now-mended heart,
*   a cherished priceless treasure,*
Pieces put back together again
*   turned the mourning to a joyous pleasure.*
Now transformed, this precious love
*   like an open sieve*
Poured into the basin of her heart
*   to start anew, a cleansed life to live.*

July 1, 2003

Jeremiah 31:13; Psalm 31:12;
The Cup of our Life, Rupp, Joyce, pp. 87-106

Our Advocate

In our silent loneliness
Suffering and despair
cry of anguish
when first appears
the silent awesome fears;
Our Advocate - our comforting
Helper, our amazing grace
this Healer, his loving kindness
sent to intercede
on our behalf,
all to embrace.
The balm of oil
soothe to heal
the Good Samaritan
freely given -
poured upon the wounds -
those of us wounded victims
to the stranger's hand.
This Advocate
Son of God, freely given
in time of stressful hour
His healing power - in time of
need
tender mercies - to set us free.

February 3, 2004
1 John 2:1-2; Luke 10:30-37

A Changeable Promise

Do we view God in everything?
Constantly creating, always renewing,
Forever changeless, His Spirit regenerating
in everything, in every happening.
His creative hand unchangeable, unchanging,
Omnipotent, all powerful, Omnipresent, all being.
Together on the road of life,
      His Son our traveling companion,
      our reassuring guardian,
      our protector, chaperone.
On the road to Emmaus, closer than a friend,
      who gives the nod to walk
      this journey of spiritual growth
      together, as we listen and as we talk.
On the path of righteousness,
      of spiritual hunger and thirst;
      A willingness to let go and take the avenue of reverse.
      To feed our hunger and to quench
         our thirst for improvement,
      to be satisfied to replace
         our attitude for a rich betterment.
His unlimited love, the firm foundation of life
      rebuilds a new awareness
      in the fertile ground of goodness and humility.
      Rooted, to keep us from stumbling.
      Our spiritual act of worship rooted in
      the offering of our bodies - to free us
      from falling, to free us from complaining.
Both give power to reshape and to transform,
to create, to inspire, to reform.
Time woven through all seasons of growth
provides the promise of a changeable presence.
All selfishness released that binds,
radiates a natural sweetness, an inner acceptance,
A portrait of a Christ-like child, one of a kind.

May 11, 2003
Genesis 1; Luke 24:13-32; Jude 24; Romans 12:1-5

19

Giver of Strength

Turn to the Giver of mercy and strength
   for help and understanding.
He is your helper, keeper, and staying power,
   your comforter to increase strength every hour.
Do not heed the voice of fear
   nor turn away; His promise is assuredly near.
Lord, I believe my hope comes from your presence;
   therefore, help me not to turn a heavy ear,
But to listen to your inner voice, to hear,
   to find sustained faith from unexpected pains,
   to find the mighty reservoir of courage
Always clear, always fresh, that never drains.
Holy Spirit, quencher of thirst,
   to you alone my being yields,
   You, my refuge and my shield.
   Giver of life, quiet solace, hide yourself in me.
Remove this valley of bruised suffering and pain
as I wait for your blessing to set me free.
I claim this promise:
   "He heals the broken-hearted and
   binds up their wounds." Amen!

March 12, 2003
Isaiah 40:29; Isaiah 41:10;
Psalm 27:14; Psalm 121:1; Psalm 147:3

Expressions of Nature Prayers

The Wonderment and Beauty of our Creator,
Father God and Sustainer of all things good.

A Spring Parable

When for a little while
Wintertime of life
Presents its ear to hear
Shades of ashen gray and fright
A glimpse of failing fear.

Through the earthly soil
Spring breaks forth
Watering the earth's toil
In joyous, pleasing colors
Dressed up in spiritual truth;
Birthing fresh life, resurrection power.
Transforming renewal hope, every hour.

Flowing… "rivers of living waters"[1]
undressing, gripping dreary darkness
Into the risen Lord's holy light[2]
At last, free from winter's shades
of ashen gray, fear and fright.[3,4]

January 17, 2004

1 John 7:38
2 John 12:24
3 2 Corinthians 3:17
4 2 Corinthians 5:17

"Beauty Is"

Beauty is everything
  Everything is Beauty
Beauty is everywhere
  Everywhere is Beauty
Beauty is powerful
  Powerful is Beauty
Beauty is nature
  Nature is Beauty
Beauty is "Is"
  "Is" is Beauty
Everything, everywhere, that breathes
  "Is" expressed in human spirits
  Is praiseworthy!

1979
Psalm 50:2; Psalm 150

The Willow's Lament

Willow! By surprise you caught my eye.
 Can't remember the many times I passed you by,
Placed on earth, your life to be a weeper-tree,
 Called to be a giver, a source of empathy.
As one of life's perfect designs,
 Uniquely gifted, created by the divine
Author and Perfecter of your name -
 "Weeping Willow," no other the same.
A messenger sent from Him,
 your tears weep good news to mankind.
God of Heaven made us a world of glory,
 and honored you to tell us the story.
Clothed you to wear the beauty of your tears,
 Tall and graceful on your slender ladylike boughs.
Bending, drooping over, mourning softly, tenderly
 Moving with the gentle wind, calmly, serenely.
You bend and sway your leafy branches,
 Spilling colored tears of green,
Shedding leaves like manna descended,
 Such a humbling, touching scene.
Just as the True Bread descended from above
 Spilling living tears of brightest red,
Shedding His blood once for all
 To quench our thirst, to be spiritually fed.
Intricately made to be weepy, Willow,
 Like you, our hurts released
 and dropped on tear-stained pillows.
Just like you, our eyes pour out weeping tears.
 Day and night the tears never quit.
Weeper-Giver, your gift of tears freely giving
 Find our refuge 'neath the
 roof of your umbrella home
Under your willowy, limber branches
 - always reaching.
 Find there is a time to weep.
 Alas! And a time to laugh and roam.
Our Creator, also our Restorer
 Promises always to be with us in our weeping.
The Righteous Branch, the One, also, who wept,
 Promises to aid us to bear the seed for growing.

You meet this role weeping, giving, and healing,
 Rooted and grounded into a sensitive strength
Like you we are seeded and
 planted to go forth weeping,
 Our primary mission to
 "reap our joy through our tears."
Fallen quiet, healing tears
 down through timeless years,
 Weeping Willow, Weeper-Giver,
 cascade your compassionate tears.
Therefore, Willow Weeper,
 "Take delight in the Lord who imparts
His pleasure and His joy,
 For He will give to you the desires of your heart."
July 26, 2003
Genesis 1:12; Hebrews 12:2; John 4:10; Isaiah 53:5;
John 4:13-14; John 6:31-35; Jeremiah 14:17;
Ecclesiastes 3:4; John 11:35; John 4:29-30;
Psalm 126:5-6; Psalm 37:4

The Bleeding Heart;
Flower of Compassion

Bleeding Heart
> The Lord which called you by your name[1]
> Come! The start of a brand new day
> is on the way. Come!
> It's time to take a meditative walk
> a contemplative heart-to-heart talk.

Bleeding Heart
> Unlike your sister flowers
> not elegant, stately, flashy or rare
> you seem not to flaunt a fancy flair.
> Why is this? Can it be, 'cause
> you are old fashioned?
> Maybe timid? A wallflower, maybe? I think not!

Bleeding Heart
> The Lord of All Comfort
> gave you His compassion so that you may be able
> to show compassion to others…[2]
> Created you a quiet, showy flower
> did not give you a spirit of timidity[3]
> but a spirit of love and comfort
> spirit of self-control and power.

Bleeding Heart
> With your heart-shaped bloom
> full of holy grace
> cheeks of rosy-pink
> with a blushing face
> donned in your herbaceous blue-green foliage
> have the ability to manifest
> the quiet fears on another's breast.

From the corner of my eye, what is this?
> Tear-filled eyes, coursing down your droopy cheeks
> visibly, compassion sobbing appears
> mingles with blood and white water tears
> resemblance of the compassionate One
> outstretched, hanging naked on Friday's cross.[4]

Sympathetic flower, flower lamenting
> Like the Man acquainted with grief[5]
> you pump a light-hearted tranquility
> with your scent of deep humility
> you evoke intensive, sympathetic care
> to meet the needs of those in deep despair.

Bleeding Heart, Flower of Compassion
> always been and continue to be
> The Lord which called you by your name
> Always will remain. So like,
> His name above all names
> Jesus, with His precious blood, set us free[6]
> Alive, always been and always will be.

---

1 Genesis 1:11,12
2 2 Corinthians 1:3,4
3 2 Timothy 1:7
4 Isaiah 53:5
5 Isaiah 53:3
6 Isaiah 9:6

Dear Lord, our time spent together
> In the quiet of this early morn;
> as sun's golden light, arises to be born
> hear my ardent heartfelt prayer; Thank you -
> for the gift of tears, that kissed me in the rain
> for, how, you taught my feeble faith
> to flower, to grow and to bloom.

Singing lips of praise and glory[7]
> My Lord, I pray, thank you
> for your blessed grace
> poured upon my face today;
> for your beloved Son, Redeemer, Friend
> for your bleeding, glory flower
> both, just a heartbeat away.

Bleeding Heart, lend a listening ear
> The God of Mercy, our breaking hearts
> hears our lamenting cries.
> In heaven's garden when next we meet
> His tender, caring hands
> more than a mother's tender heart
> will wipe away every sorrow[8]
> every silent sighs
> and every tear from our earthly eyes.[9]

May 1, 2005

---

7 Psalm 63:3,4
8 Isaiah 35:10
9 Revelation 21:4

Bird of Fire

How does the Holy Spirit its Person tell?
  Spread out, White Bird, mighty of radiant light
Slender of wing, descend your heavenly flight
  Pour down your presence from high above
Transcend your work, your source of power
  Abide within our being, your Person for each hour.

Come, Paraclete, your flame of fire-red, descend upon our hearts
  Come, Holy Comforter, come alongside to comfort and guide
To lead, to teach your tender love and grace
  To make our hearts your sacred dwelling place
To bring the message of your truth and light
  Take hold now our hearts, use us, Spirit of life.

Sound of Judgment, as the rush of a wind's sound
  Search us, grant us your counsel, mightily abound
On burners of our heart, consume all iniquities
  As the deer pants for the waters, brooks… revive, refresh,
  quench our thirst, remove all partialities
Spiritually to grow, for by your Spirit to be aglow!

Breath of the Almighty, breathe softly over our hearts;
  to show the fruits of your spirit… kindness, peace, self-control.
Your sensitive, innocent Person, the Savior to glorify
  Transform us into a life anew, altars of living sacrifice
Help us to believe, ready us to receive; spring
  Streams of living water, fullness of plenty bring.

On the tablets of our hearts, brand your mark upon us
  Bring to completion your seal of guarantee
Highlight these Spirit signs clearly to see
  "Not by might nor by power, but by your Spirit."
You, the Third Person, Holy Spirit, for each hour,
  Our helper, the love of God, poured out in our hearts.

1975

Acts 2:1; John 16:13-14; Job 32:8; Ephesians 3:20;
Psalm 42:1-2; Romans 12:11; Galatians 5:22;
Zechariah 4:6; John 7:38-39; Romans 5:5

My Day Lily

Good morning, Day Lily
  in this serene, quiet time
My friend, I bid you a cheery welcome.
  I greet the beauty of your
  glowing, bright, yellow face
  I watch your sleepy arms outstretched
  towards the sun's light gaze.
Enjoy your day, dear friend
  in His glowing light.
Enjoy your happy play
  with earth's life delight.
Your Creator-Maker dressed you
  in your Sunday's best -
  to give to me, to others, a time to refresh.
He gave to you alone, your own unique name
  to bring your expression of
  comfort, joy, tenderness of grace
  to lighten up those fragile of face.
That smile upon your inner soul
  most I cherish
  the memory to linger, never to perish.
I pray Lord, a heart full of thanks
  for this precious friend
  you so unselfishly gave,
  to lift the human spirit's maze.
Always, with your mighty power
  there, to bind the wounds of hurts
  with your healing, needed flower.
With your nice warm feeling inside,
  dear Lily, I bid you goodnight.
Your daily work well done,
  always faithful, loving, having fun.
God's blessings upon you, friend,
  always loyal, laughing, trusting, true.
Sleep sweetly now, covered over with protective dew
See you in the early morn - on time
  to renew our secret friendship,
  to heal, to cheer each other most sublime.

1975
Genesis 1; Matthew 6:28,29

A Sunflower Blessing

Lord God, Creator from the beginning,
from your jewel box of nature
you made a common flower
with a "good morning" face,
To greet us daily with abundant grace.
A sunflower with a bright funny smile,
an infectious, glowing personality
to shine forth a cheerfulness, a light gaiety,
bringing warmth to the inner soul.
Like the sunburst in a jewel brooch
shooting rays of brilliant light,
you grant our hearts delight.
Sunflower, in your childish way,
your clownish ruffled-trimmed face
full of mischief, full of fun,
You stand tall on your lanky frame,
towering over barefaced virgin leaves.
All seem to evoke feelings of merry play.
You seem to say, "This is the Lord's day.
Rejoice and be glad in it."
Sunflower seeder, your head - bearing seeds
scattered upon the soil of our hearts,
sowing the Lord's word of truth.
Spreading love, joy, and laughter,
bearing seeds of fruit forever after.
Your soothing oil-of-gladness
washes every sorrow away
curing the chronic pain of sadness.
Oh! Lord our Creator, Maker,
from your heaven's gate
you heard our cheerless, sunless cries
deep within the alcove of our soul.
You sent the genesis of the flower in the sun
to smile upon us,
to make Your face to shine upon us,
to keep us with your keeping power,
to give us lasting peace for every hour.
Thank you, gracious Lord,
for the benediction of
your sunflower blessing.
Hail! Friendly, beloved sunflower.
You bring a blessing to our souls
with your whimsical face.
You have a beauty all your own,
an eye-catching, orange-yellow jewel.
You leave a legacy of heavenly treasures,

a keepsake of precious,
everlasting pleasures.
You were born to glorify our Lord.
To Him be the praise,
the honor,
and the glory.
For you, sunflower, we will greatly rejoice
and have fun in your
Maker's creative morning sun.

August 1, 2005

Genesis 1:1-5; Psalm 118:24; Luke 8:11;
Galatians 5:22; Psalm 45:1-8; Numbers 6:24,25

As White as the New-Fallen Snow

Dear Father God, my Creator, so great,
Silence within hears your low, still voice;
Hear you softly, so sweetly talking to me,
through the silence so deep,
through the quiet of thee,
Through the soul of the newly-born snow.
My Spirit so free raced to your presence,
Raced to have sweet communion with thee.
So eager to come as one with you,
we both stepped into and through
the purity and whiteness of
your new-fallen world.
Lost in the oneness, this snow, you and I,
enjoyed our creative and heavenly peace,
Arms lifted high in adoration,
praising you, the ever-creating Master;
for this beauty created a wondrous work,
so good, so perfect, beyond understanding.
This beauty of whiteness, purity clean,
sensing within your plan and your scheme;
A whiteness, a purity that lights the way
To the core of your snow,
to the core of my heart.
This purity, this whiteness,
        to me you impart
To change to radiant light
        the unhappy dark.
To wash and to cleanse,
        every sin to pass on,
to change death back to life once again
The breath of life felt,
        melting this old mold.
The breath of your warmth
        felt through the chill of the cold;

through this sense of warmth.
Oh, take my soul, tenderly,
        sweetly to wash and cleanse,
        my Lord.
This hurt of darkness,
        this deep hurt of pain
With the whiteness of
        your new-born snow
To be left with the sense
        of cleanness so fresh,
so soothing, comforting
        to the soul of my being.
I rejoice in your precious,
        oh, holy, place,
as I feel the blanket
        of whiteness cover me o'er.
My soul's longing satisfied
        as we walk hand-in-hand
into eternal silence,
        into each snowflake born;
each new snowflake soft, so clean;
each His own slowly falls;
to gather more, to pass into time,
        to live for ever and evermore.
With each fallen flake
        I draw even nearer still,
To enjoy a rapture that your arms instill.
Just to feel one single flake upon my heart
is to know "how great Thou art."
Caught up in the wide
        open heavens of white
layered snow, expressing
        your truth, expressing your love.
I place myself now to follow your steps;

the imprint of whiteness leads me to strength.
This strength of new freshness,
        my soul lifted high;
I'm drawn into oneness of glory and light.
My soul gives praise and thanks for
showing your love, forgiving love made
of heavenly light. A purity of whiteness,
to make me aware our transgressions,
All sins, you will take in and bear.
How good this completeness, to be made a part
of your new-born snow; fallen so perfect,
so good; fallen so clean from your own
holy heart. Creator, Master, Father, my God,
your sermon of forgiving, healing love
goes as deep as the snow, as deep as my
prayer, as white as a born-me-again soul.
I respond to your voice within me, to say,

"Now let us reason together, you and I."
Though your sins are like scarlet, they
shall be as white as this new-born
fallen snow.
Lost in the warm embrace of this
new-soft snow, the depth of this
prayer you have heard;
With assurance of joy, my soul
I just know; be still, oh, my soul,
I just know.

Wednesday January 7, 1976

How Great Thou Art, Stuart K. Hine, 1899
1 John 1:9; Isaiah 1:18-18; Psalm 51:7

Expressions of Glory Prayers

The Open Door so Everyone may enter in.
Aim for Eternal Life, there is the Cross at the End.

The Room of Love

There is a faith that stings the beat of the heart,
      an injured faith piercing as the quiver's arrow flight,
A faith that does not keep us from our many sufferings,
      a fearful faith that wounds the body's plight.
There is no room in the chambers of the heart
      for these pains of fearful, hurtful faith,
These fears of anguish, fears of loss, the fear of loneliness,
      fears of worry, the fear of others, fear of unforgiveness.
Little children, these crippling fears we need to banish.
      Our compassionate God is always there to remove the
      tarnish.
The Lord of comfort, warmth of presence, always near,
      mercifully, tenderly to meet and ease the fear.
Enter the Master's room of love, filled with the presence of
His Holy Dove,
      the artist's original.
       "There is no fear in love."
This believing faith makes things
happen; nothing will be impossible.
      Faith stands at the door, knocks,
      says "do not fear, open,
      come on in."
This One, wounded, endured, prevailed,
      stretched upon The Wood
      offers spiritual food to feed and
shape our life for good.
Hear His voice of truth, remove the fear,
      embrace the pain
      In His room of love,
      health restored, health regained.
      His room filled with the
      indwelling Holy Dove —
our Comforter, our Guide, Our Love.

April 5, 2003

1 John 4:18,19; John 16:12-15;
Revelation 3:20; Matthew 8:10-13;
Matthew 17:20,21

The Lamb: The Way of Escape

"Who is without blemish?"
      Not I! There is not one,
Only the Lamb, perfect, spotless,
         who hangs from the tree,
Robe dipped in blood, perfectly sinless.
Why do you ask,
        "Why did He have to die?"
For you and me -
        our sins freely forgiven once for all
To dry the eyes for all who cry.
The Lamb of God,
       Who shed His blood
       set out on the narrow back-way road,
       on a humble donkey rode,
Looked neither to the left nor to the right.
 Though in His peripheral sight
       saw the heinous acts -
          party time!
Brothers, sisters acting up,
sinning wild - morally vile,
quarreling, thievery abounds
         lustfully carousing around.
Further along the charted way He went,
      turned into the horseshoe bend,
      there, leaning on their own evil ways,
      wandering far astray,
      lost on their own roadways,
      His children. He weeps as He prays.
Traveled the world wide
to the crest of hills,
Looked over the sides,
floundering in valleys of tears,
wept to see gaunt faces full of fears,
The multitudes of loneliness
living in their misery,
in their pain of bitterness,
lost in their own applause.
"Why did He have to die?" Because!

His heavenly Father looked down,
spent out His own compassion -
wanted His beloved children
back home again, to their heavenly mansion.
Sent His beloved One to reconcile
His children from their morbid vile,
to send them back where they belonged,
their accepted inheritance sealed,
to those who received, to those who believed.
You see, He, Our Victor, deliberately
conquered death, evil deeds
To turn the tears of our cries
into eternal rainbow skies.
This is why He died - for no one
goes to His Father except through
the slaughtered Lamb, His Son.
He provided the way of escape,
Our Redeemer Lord.
I know, because I was there
at the foot of the cross.
It was for you and for me
that He died.
He told me so - it is true!
As He cradled me in His arms,
He will also cradle you.
As the angels sing His praises,
to His holy name.
In song let's lift up our voices,
and sing, Worthy is the Lamb.

May 7, 2004

Proverbs 3:5,6; 2 Corinthians 4:17,18;
2 Corinthians 10:13; Revelation 5:11-13;
Isaiah 6:3

Easter Morn

Bless the Lord
    who lived, loved, and died -
    Indeed, buried, arose again, bodily alive.
Bless His Holy name,
    He who is our righteousness
    Died for our unrighteousness.
    He who is holy
    Died for our unholiness.
    He who is just,
    Did He not die for our injustice?
    "…in this while we were yet sinners,
    He died for us."
In His Blessed hour
    He, who is honored and loved,
    Our King and Beloved One,
    His work upon the cross well done.
    "It is finished!" Alleluia! O, Praise Him!
    New life now has begun.

In His Victorious hour
    Died once for all - not twice,
    On the cross, through the nail
    we, all, bought at a costly price.
    Now, entrance through the split veil,
    Extolling trumpets, resounding horn.
    The morning's herald call:
    "The risen glory of the Cross."

Hello! Welcome, happy Easter morn;
Surely, everlasting Hope is born.

April 20, 2003

Romans 5:8; Matthew 27:50,51;
John 19:30; Luke 24:6-8

About the Man and the Cross

Why do I love you? Lord, Savior, Mine
   You first loved me.[1]
   I know your love is true
   like streams of living waters[2]
   a love that freely flows from you.
Lamb of God, whom we long offended
   in your courageous silence[3]
   unblemished without sin[4]
   outstretched, wounded hands
   by your blood, the agony and shame
   freely purchased me;
   bore the punishment for my sins[5]
   bruised for my transgressions
   where I was to blame.

O, Jesus, my King Eternal
   Why do I love you? For me,
   you wore a crown of plaited thorns[6]
   placed upon your head
   worn with great nobility.
   No kingly robe; donned only
   in your raiment
   clothes worn in great humility.
   Still yet, your lowly garb
   when pierced, mocked, disgraced,
   you showed yourself more splendidly.
   Jesus, a carpenter's son
   lifted up your hammered grace[7]
   my will in conflict with yours
   nailed it to the face
   of the old wooden beam.
   Redemptive stripes – both hope and glory[8]
      to make me pure
      to heal me sure

to make me a priesthood holy.[9] How do I
   love you, Lord? I love Thee[10]
   with my whole heart, soul and mind[11]
unceasingly, persistently in a quiet way
with a burning passion centered
in the chamber's heart; with all my strength
a fierce love, hidden away.

continued...

How could I not love you?
　My Savior, Redeemer, Friend
　Your willingness to give yourself for me
　Yourself, to become as such
　as one like me (human)
　Your forgiving, healing love
　tender mercies, compassionate love
　visible on the naked cross
　for all mankind to see.
　You pose the question
　　When did I first love Him?
　　Where do you ask?
At the footstool of the cross
Tear-stained cheeks upward looked
There, behind those pain-filled eyes
revealed a love for me beyond compare.
A helpless victim I became.
It was love at first sight.
　　Thou knows that I love thee, Lord.[12]
Love your name, Jesus - Name
　　above all names.
The lonely night, the hour of darkness
turned into a day of brightness
a garden of glorious gladness.
Where, when once a sinner, confessed
　　now freed from the bondage of sin
　　became reborn.
Where, did I first believed[13]
　　now became transformed.

His gift of saving grace[14]
　precious, undeserving I received.
Where, I fell deeply in love with Him
　Jesus, my Lover, My Beloved
　Why do I say,
　I can't quite stop loving Him.
Jesus, Lover of my soul[15]
　He is precious to me
　more precious than pure gold.
　Love Him for His selflessness
　hears the cry of my helplessness.
His devoted intimacy in and with His Father
　In the beginning became the WORD.[16]
　The WORD became flesh
　dwelled among us… beheld His glory
　begotten of the Father,
　　full of grace and truth.[17]
　The mystery of His deity, too profound
　to comprehend, incomprehensible,
　　divinely renowned.
How grateful a heart.
　Thank you my Redeemer, Lord,
　　Son of thy Father
　for your atoning work upon the cross
　for pouring out your
　　compassionate heart
for coming to do what I could not do myself
　Victorious, your work finished, well done
　victory over the grave won
　conquered, destroyed the evil one
　　the bruising of His heel
　　bruised the serpent head.[18]
　Thank you beautiful Savior,
　　for the tearing-open veil[19,20]
　the barrier, my sins taken away.
　　Thy will has been done.
Now, access to the throne of grace[21]
　entrance into the
　　　　　　　　　　　　continued…

Father's domain (Kingdom)
into His reconciled glory place
to share our joy, face to face
Holy, Holy,
  Holy Lord of Hosts, angels sing
Holy Spirit, Spirit of God,
    take my hand[22]
lead me to my eternal temple home,
  as was planned.
About the Man and the Cross
Like long ago, a pilgrim passer-by[23]
Simon, the man of Cyrene
no thought of harm to self
compelled to shoulder the Cross of Grace
weary, solely alone, His body bruised
under the weight too heavy to bear
The Cyrenian had the honor of
fellowship with Him to share.
Though heavy be our cross to bear
the Bread of life, our compassionate Christ
His living presence, healing power always there.
When we a bitter bread to eat, stress and strain[24]
a plate of aches and pains, sorrow and fear
upon His tender bosom breast
our souls within to rest;
He offers us a better Bread,
So like the passer-by long ago
the honor of fellowship with Him we share
Yes! It's about the Man and the Cross
  His life, agony and death
  His new created life
  Jesus, the Crucified Man, the Galilean
  A Man of Sorrows, for if we suffer with Him
  we shall also reign with Him forever.[25]
Son of God, Son of Man,
True God, True Man, completed the task
  The Christ, a new resurrection life[26]
  in our hearts now lives — free of the past[27]

stained with sin no more
  He has put all our sins behind His back.[28]
Jesus, His burial, our burial — nailed our
  sins to the cross
Now it is finished! Now is the hour![29]
God's divine plan, God's divine purpose
used His son's resurrection power
to bring us back to where we belong.

  This Jesus, the Nazarene[30]
  This Jesus, the Man of Galilee

February 1, 2005

1. John 4:10
2. John 7:38
3. Isaiah 53:7
4. Isaiah 53:5
5. Matthew 27:27-30
6. Mark 15:16-20
7. 1 Peter 2:24
8. 1 Peter 2:25
9. 1 Peter 2:9
10. *Sonnets from the Portuguese*, Elizabeth Barrett Browning, p. 52, 1993.
11. Deuteronomy 6:5,6
12. John 21:15-17
13. Romans 12:1-2
14. Ephesians 2:8-9
15. *Jesus, Lover of My Soul*, Charles Wesley, 1736
16. John 1:1-2
17. John 1:14
18. Genesis 3:15
19. John 15:37-38
20. Hebrews 9:1-8
21. Romans 5:2
22. Romans 8:14
23. Mark 15:21
24. Matthew 11:28-30
25. 1 Peter 4:12,13
26. Galatians 2:20
27. 2 Corinthians 5:17
28. Isaiah 38:17
29. John 19:30
30. Matthew 2:22,23

A Time for Christmas Things

Good Times, crying times, giving and receiving times
…a time for celebrating, family and friends
…a time for sharing, loved ones most dear
Special sharing with ones in need and want,
        not too far, but very near.
 First Christmas birth, remembered Holy things
…a time to open room in the heart's abode
… to hear the cries from stressful desolation
…a time to feel the pain, the sorrows of tribulation
To be a strength to the weak under Your sheltered wings.
I say to you, "Is it not the time to provide those
…a precious gift of hope and grace born from above
…a time to minister compassion, empathy and warmth
        deeply grounded in fertile soil of His love
This Emmanuel - God with us."
Holy dwelling place, Your place of home
…for all to access forgiveness, all to roam
…sent to heal the brokenhearted;
 Lord, attend to my need to help, to teach, the things of Your grace
Now, is the time to seek the lost and lonely,
        the hurting human race.
…this time, Christmastime, Holy time
…this time is now to tell the story,
The Christmas things of Jesus and His glory.

Luke 2:1-13; Isaiah 7:14; Isaiah 9:6
Christmas 2002

By His Design

In the poor little village of Nazareth in Galilee
Anne, the woman of the House of David, she,
    a part of God's sovereign plan,
predestined from the beginning of time.
    Her womb opened, she was great with
    child,
conceived and purified by God's design, by His
    demands,
    the child engraved on the palms of His
    hands.
His infinite goodness and His love
    saw fit for Anne
to mother the Mother of God,
    the high honor shown her from above.
To house her second-born child, a boy not to be.
    The sole intent, another girl,
    called by Her name, "Mary."
Chosen before her birth, "The Lord is with thee."
    Blessed, full of grace, full of faith, and
    glory.
There are times when we are
    meant not to understand
Times meant to believe, to steadfast stand
    For His divine ways
    are beyond (always) ours.
He never chooses like natural man
    His promises always keeping
    His promises never breaking
    His timing always a reason
    His using Anne for a definite season.
Because of the part
    Anne was to play,
the coming of the Anointed One
    was the only way!
Anne and Mary, knitted together
    from Him, found great favor.
    Upon them, His Spirit came
    to bless two women both the same,

    To use them in their own unique ways.
Both to carry His plan divine,
    to bring good news to all,
    about the True Vine.
Each called to fulfill the plan, to be used
    as we are called to spread the news.
The hand of God -
    Designer, Planner, drew up the Plan.
This Mary, the Mother of God,
    Virgin Mother of Jesus, and
    Anne, the Mother of Mary,
    this grandmother of Jesus
    All according to His purpose
    That was the secret plan!

April 30, 2003

John 20:16; Matthew 1:18-25; Luke 4:18;
Isaiah 49:16; Luke 1:28;
Romans 4:21; Romans 8:28;
Unafraid by Francine Rivers (2001),
pp 10, 11, 209, 210

Just a Spot of Green

Hear me, Lord, my Creator-Maker
    Make me to be more like you
    An oasis, just "a spot of green"
    To shepherd those in pastures, barren sinners
    without a spot of green
who feed on a don't bother me thirsty land
wandering, lost in a dry, parched, barren wasteland.
Lord, Washer of feet, you ask, "Do you know what I have done to you?"[1]
    Make me to be a basin, a humble servant, Lord
    such as the likes of you, meek and lowly
    Make me pouring water, that I should do what you did for me,
    thoroughly, to wash the soles of another's feet
    dirt smeared, unclean, soiled bare feet.
    Gird me with your forgiving snow-white towel[2]
    to wipe away the tainted stains of worldly sin.

O Jesus, my Refresher Friend
    Make me a sheltered cove, a spiritual retreat
    I need your refuge, to hide myself in you
    And for those, thirsty for a hiding place of shade
    Take hold of us Lord, move your Spirit-hand
    pass over us who harbor rags of sin
    pour down your mercy from above
    slather us with your soothing, healing love.

Heaven-sent Redeemer,
    How great your love for us, you heard our cry
    From heaven you descended
    Opened up your floodgates of heaven
    Came down to wash away
    our unwashed ragged sins.
        Rich blessings pouring[3]
        Rich blessings overflowing
        no longer just a spot of green. Rejoice!
        Pastures forever, full of sweet abundant joy.
        I understand, Lord
        heard your voice...[4]

1 John 13:1-20
2 Isaiah 1:18; Psalm 51:7
3 Malachi 3:10
4 Psalm 116:1

You came that we might have life[5]
and have it more abundantly.
You have placed before us an open door[6]
an invitation for fellowship restored.
"Through my gate, verily, verily," I heard you say.
"If anyone enters by me, he will be saved."[7]
He will be cared for, and will go in and out
find joy and fruitful pasturelands.
For, I am always there with open, loving hands.
June 1, 2005

5 John 10:10
6 Revelation 3:8 (The Message)
7 John 10:9

Epilogue

Through my many years living in intensive suffering, the sovereign hand of the Father chastened me to be refined and purified. Through baptismal waters, I resurrected into a new-born creation. A spiritual transformation soon became a way of life for me in Christ. How He changed my life! He made me whole; He became real for me.

Kindly I say, dear reader, that He cares deeply for you. In your own call of suffering, He alone is your encouragement. He is your ALL comfort. He showers you with His keeping faith through His saving grace. Cast all your cares upon Him. His mercies have no boundaries.

Thank you, dear reader, for the privilege of entering into your private, sacred struggles. Let us together match our cries of tears and travel the road of THIS Jesus, our abiding joy and Healer-Restorer.

Personal Remarks

Purposely, the following writing was saved for the last which truly was the beginning; to give you, the reader a better view of how suffering turned into a blessing. For me, long were the many years of suffering on the bed of affliction. The pain took me into the quiet silence of my being where God heard my helpless plea. No pain is too great that God does not bring a measure of comfort and some kind of resurrection.

For me, He embraced my plea and brought me to HIMSELF through the avenue of Christ; the Calvary scene made into a Blessing. "Therefore, if anyone who is in Christ, He is a new creation; the old has passed away, Behold! The new has come" (2 Corinthians 5:17).

Expression Endings

Behold My Friend – Pain

You were a stranger and you took me in. You were a stranger and you wanted my self to be your friend. You being a stranger, the self of me wanted no parts of the being of you. I asked, then pleaded; finally a beggar I became, begging your leave, to pass me by. The I of me wanted you not; your friendship needed I not. Unable to flee your presence, you became determined in your want. How I feared you! A threat to my freedom; you limited my going and coming. My "being" began to sense the power of your possessiveness. Slowly, gradually, creeping into the cells of consciousness, into the cells of my body, mind and spirit. I ran from you, unable to free my "self" from your power-You see, you were to me a stranger. I never knew your kind. I did not want to take you in. I felt you were an enemy, out to seek and torment, to destroy the I of me. Your friendship tore into the inner core of my consciousness. My spirit, body you filled with fears. I found your will to be deep and lonely. Your will that gnawed with strength, to pierce the heart with blood of agony and tears. I watched the way your will gave birth to stings and bites. To mold and cut and bruise – You were to me the worst of all my enemies. The I of me unable, could not see your love, your comfort, your table, so how could you feed me? Your home so dark and, oh, so cold. The self of me hungry so for light to understand, to understand the why of you. You, who was sent to choose me for your friend. How could we relate? We, who had in common not a thing? We were total strangers, you and I. Behold, the realization for each other illuminated itself into the souls of our being. We felt the need to love. The soul of you, dear pain, and the soul of me embraced. It could not stop, your pain-of-love, my love-to-pain. Together we yielded to every cell our thoughts, to every cell our actions. The I of me surrendered to the will of you. I took you in, you became my master; you took me in, I became your slave. United we were, no longer strangers but now as one. To go through wondrous journeys together, you and I.

You slowly showed me you were never against me, but were always for me. You were truly my friend, sent to me by only Him, to be chosen. I soon sensed the strength of your power, the light of your wisdom, guiding my thoughts, changing my acts. Your desires were soon mine. My desires were yours, and all these desires seek to manifest in goodness. The process of you, my friend, began a good work in me. Your knowledge of me, buried so deep, your friendship, raised my soul's longing for life, my soul's longing for love. My new found love, for you no longer hurt, replaced, instead with abundant joy. No longer cold, a warmth emerged, a sweetness of love overflowed into life-penetrating, the living-creating part of my self.

I found myself drawing closer to you, the breath of my soul listening to the beat of your heart. The self of me became very still, quickly to find your secret hid, especially for me. You whispered softly a mystery for me. You whispered again and again, "Be still, my soul. Be still and know. Then you will know." "Know what! Know who! Know why?" came my reply. You labored with me, listened I to you; you walked with me, and talked to me. We became one from two. You in me and I in you. You, patiently waiting; I, patiently watching. Unaware, at first, your way was foreign to me. In clear amazement; travail came forth. A well sprung up and poured love, love divine, flowing around my being.

My friend, beloved, so dear, assigned to be His helper, near! He could penetrate my All, through you alone, for me to find His haven home. My self expanded wider still and the I of me turned completely in; with absolute faith and trust, I allowed expression of your birth to do my thinking and creative work. All three of us were partners now. Our Father's work in his house would be done. Glory of Glories, blessings hidden were mine revealed!

continued...

How could I be made to recognize my Father God?

His very expression of life, spoken to the true understanding of love?

How could I be made to realize the total essence of life?

How could I be made to soar so high, to heights of spiritual renewal?

How could I be made to find The Giver-Maker, the source of life?

How could I be made to find the Eternal Healer, His divine source of power, found within the eternal core of my being?

Oh, how could I be made, dear friend, to feel the spirit of my soul? To know the I of me was born in the I of Him, my Creator, His image and His likeness; and to know all things He created and He saw that it was all good.

Oh, how, dear friend, could the eyes-of-my soul see His love and compassion, so tender, so gentle? How could I be made to understand this love, given for all mankind, given through the blood of His precious Son?

How, dear friend, without you at my side? Without you in my side? Your tender-taste sweet-sweet pain, your hot wet tears, turned to pearls; your constant fire burning joy, joy of comfort, inner strength. There was no other way for me; I know your way alone, you chose me forevermore. Disguised and masked you gave your all; your life for me, laid down your all. And the I of me dared to love you all! But now, my dear, beloved friend, we both know the time has come. That you must leave and I must part. No longer do we have the need for each other's heart. Your purpose, which was His, has been fulfilled; your work of perfection has been done.

You and I, our pain, has borne a oneness unique for such as us; as we walked the road of Jericho, hand in hand, no longer strangers, You and I.

I did not choose you, not I; you found me lost along life's way. Your still small voice inside, to me so softly said, I was He and He was I. We live together, He and I together, in my soul. I heard softly said again, "He is that I of me, He is my all, He is mine divine."

We learned to love each other, you and I. But now you were free, released to go. I bid you well, my friend, dear, dear friend. I will not say good-bye; for we will surely meet again to cross each other's paths, in friendly recognition, our needs to be met again.

Go now, dear friend, go quickly as I brush away sweet tears. The memory of you will gradually fade, but the love for you, I place within my heart.

I was a stranger and "you" took me in. Your expression of pain led me to your perfect expression of love. My true friend; the light, the way, the truth and life.

Nov. 5, 6, 7, 1975

Genesis 1:27; Genesis 1:31; 2 Peter 4:12-13; 2 Peter 5:10-11; John 14:5-6; 2 Corinthians 4:16-17; John 8:12; John 11:25-26

The End in the Beginning

In our endings
        find a brand-new beginning.
In our new beginnings
        seek for another new ending.
For in these endings and beginnings
        was the Word.
"The Word was with God
        …in the beginning, the Word; the Lord."
The Lord (the Word) became flesh.
        Declaring the end in the beginning
        "…who dwelt among us,
        beheld His glory… of the Father."
At the break of dawn, the beginning of day one,
        everything "He made beautiful in its time,
        also put eternity within man's mind.
How can we know what He has done…?"
 "From the beginning to the end"
        created by Him a new dawning day
To dine on His beauties of
        mercy and grace
        Scriptures communicate
        His truths to embrace.
"I am the Omega
        the first and the last
The beginning and the end,"
        The end contained in
                the beginning; and,
From the beginning
        I went before you, was with you,
        never left you
For I am the Word made flesh,
        the spoken Word,
        The eternal living Word -
        your Lord until the end.

July 10, 2003

John 1:1-3,14; Genesis 1:1;
Isaiah 46:10; Ecclesiastes 3:11;
Revelation 21:6; Revelation 22:13

About the Author

Amelia Brumm, was born and raised in a small mill-town in Western Pennsylvania. Her life includes four careers. In her personal life, she voluntarily enlisted and served over three years in the United States Navy service during the Korean Conflict as a teletype operator in communications. She is a charter member of Women in the Military Service for America and is registered in the Women's Memorial in Arlington, Virginia. Upon her discharge, she devoted her life to being a full-time wife and mother of two adopted infant children. Later, in her professional life, she graduated from Michigan State University with a degree in Social Work. As a social worker in the Department of Family Social Services she worked in the field as an intake caseworker, counseling and student intern clinical instructor. Today Amelia is pursuing a fourth career as a first-time author. As a retired social worker, involved in the sufferings of others as well as her own personal years of suffering, she has committed herself to reaching out to those in their times of need. Her expressions of prayer written through the art of poetry are simplistic, however, profound*ly rooted in biblical scriptural references. With her husband, Dr. Lynn F. Brumm, Amelia resides in East Lansing, Michigan.*

To order additional copies of

The Voice *of the* Healer

Then and Now

Have your credit card ready and call:

1-877-421-READ (7323)

or please visit our web site at
www.pleasantword.com

Also available at:
www.amazon.com
and
www.barnesandnoble.com